Five Political Poems

by

Don Taylor

FIRST WRITES

First Writes Publications London 1994

By the same author

Stage plays

Grounds for Marriage Traverse Theatre 1967
Sisters Northcott Theatre 1968
Sam Foster Comes Home Glasgow Citizens Theatre 1969
The Roses of Eyam Northcott Theatre 1970. Samuel French 1976
The Exorcism Comedy Theatre 1975. Samuel French 1981
Out on the Lawn Watford Palace Theatre1975
A Long March to Jerusalem Watford 1976. Samuel French 1978
The Achurch Letters Greenwich Theatre 1978
When the Actors Come Wythenshawe Theatre 1979
Brotherhood Orange Tree Theatre 1986
Daughters of Venice Waterman's Arts Centre 1991. Samuel French 1992
Retreat From Moscow New End Theatre 1993
Women of Athens Hammersmith Polish Theatre 1993
When the Barbarians Came New End Theatre 1994

Translations

The Theban plays of Sophocles - Oedipus the King, Oedipus at Colonus, Antigone. Methuen 1986
The War plays of Euripides - Iphigenia at Aulis, The Women of Troy, Helen. Methuen 1990

Musicals, as lyricist, with Ellen Dryden and Charles Young.

The Burston Drum, Waterman's Arts Centre 1988. Samuel French 1989
Summer in the Park Waterman's Arts Centre 1990. Samuel French 1991.

Autobiography

Days of Vision Methuen 1986

Contents

1

First Writes Publications, London 1994

First published in 1994
by First Writes Publications
46 Maldon Road Acton W3 6SZ

Bound by Chalfont Bookbinders
Chalfont St Peter
Buckinghamshire

ISBN 0 9524159 0 9

Under the Barbarians

Today the barbarians came.
Their arrival wasn't unexpected.
For years we had talked about them, prepared
To resist, or, in some cases, conspired
To open secluded gates to them in secret.
Today they are here, but from an unsuspected
Direction, where we anticipated no threat.
We cheer, to hide our shame.

We expected the face of evil
To wear a different expression, hair
Like the Goths, knotted and greasy,
Pitiless eyes. We were queasy
With fear, as they knocked at our front door.
Our demonologies had made it quite clear
What to expect. But on the doorstep we saw
Another kind of devil.

The truth we try to hide,
Particularly from ourselves, is the embarrassing fact
That we asked them to come. They were clean,
Bright-haired, their eyes shone
With a cavernous sincerity.
They spoke politely, dressed with tact.
Their solutions charmed us with their simplicity.
No wonder we asked them inside.

Already they've been here a week,
And the parties are still going on in the houses
Of their long-time supporters. *Barbarians*
At last! they cry, *real barbarians,*
Who mean to destroy things, dismiss Congresses,
Pull down statues, rip the blouses
Of the vestal virgins, and rape the Priestesses!
The rest of us hardly dare speak.

We expected them to run mad
With pillage and terror; we turned keys,
Shot bolts, and trembled in our parlours.
But nothing happened, no security men, prowlers
Or denunciations in the papers. The old
Religion was abolished, of course, and these
Steely new Gods of theirs proclaimed.
But, really, it wasn't so bad.

Being Barbarians, their creed
Is barbarism, naturally. But what
Exactly does that mean? Are they
Different from us in any significant way?
They share one's hotel, drink at the same bar.
Yes indeed, it's a question of values: they're not
Civilised, as we are, not exactly. But so far
I haven't seen anyone bleed.

And however we split hairs
Morally and intellectually, the majority
Cheered them all the way to the Capitol
Like Conquerors, or redeemers, come to make all
Things new. That we poets and thinkers had long
Ago consigned them to the dustbin of history
Is a measure of how far we could be wrong.
Our future now is theirs.

The barbarians' first year
Was celebrated privately by initiates.
We are beginning to get used to them: the emptiness
Of their rhetoric, the shallowness
Of their thought. Intelligent people joke
About them at parties. But their conviction creates
An unpleasant atmosphere, like tobacco smoke.
We begin to comprehend fear.

We know it can't last.
We are a civilised country; for centuries
A byword for tolerance, universal sanctuary
For the exiled and oppressed. A sense of community,
A city that is its people, is the idea
We have given to the world. Such destinies
Have roots, foundations. They can't simply disappear
Overnight, like the past.

Over two hundred years
We have educated our rulers, taught the rich
To understand their dependence on the poor,
And that naked power solves nothing. I'm sure
Having assimilated the Normans, outgrown Feudalism
And constitutionalised our Kings, we shall teach
These barbarians too that their barbarism
Is no business of ours.

So what makes my hands shake?
The confident talk in restaurants and bars
Continues as before, even louder perhaps,
More strident. No intellectual collapse
That I can see. But at evening, yesterday,
Strange shadows fell across my face like scars.
Something has gone wrong. Is it we or they
Who have made a mistake?

The great barbarian war
Was fought on television. Carriers heaved
In the sitting room, young men in fighters
Were counted out and back, the red tatters
Of a Welshman's leg drew an audience of millions.
What truth beyond the image? No one believed
The jingo, but the spectacle cost billions.
Horrified, we lusted for more.

And when we looked at the mirror
Whose was the face in the glass? A Byron,
An Egmont? Or a schoolboy, thrilled
By the adventure of someone else being killed?
A grinning war mask with painted cheeks
Stamping and howling for the destruction
Of the laughable enemy. What shrieks,
In the nightmare dark! What horror!

And then the morning after,
All the shame of victory, the knowledge,
Not slowly emerging, but known from the start
That the wicked Queen had a wicked heart
And had cast these spells to preserve her beauty
By the magic of shedding blood. All that courage,
All that pain, a mere cosmetic, history
Reduced to paint and powder.

The smell of barbarian rule
Was on everyone's breath: celebration
In the Yahoo press - *Why should we pray
For dead foreigners!* - and the inevitable day
When the lies began to emerge, like rats
From their sewage and cellars. The contagion
Spread, till the tokens were on our hearts.
They had infected us all.

The art of civilised lying
Was the textbook the Greeks never wrote, their rational
Sensibilities seeing no virtue in untruth.
Logical argument, rhetorical persuasion, both
Legitimate accomplishments: but deliberately to deceive
As a matter of policy, could any national
Leader or private citizen believe
In such a fearful thing -

Barbarians excepted,
Of course - ? They were always beyond the pale
Of decent behaviour, jabbering a gibberish
Beneath civilised men, an outlandish
Corrupted babble, essentially un-Greek.
What would they think of this slippery, brutal
Concealed and concealing language we speak,
All truth self-destructed

What seems an age ago,
When the Barbarians came? The lie political,
Personal, tactical, the unyielding hammering
Of persistent untruth, is their art of persuading.
Like bent coppers who force us to sign
False confessions, they finally compel
Our consent by sheer repetition. We resign,
Acquiesce, or let go

From sheer weariness.
So now we live with the public lie,
The corrupt proceeding, the second rate
Helmsman steering the hulk of state.
We assume the untruth, not daring
To believe anymore. Something smells high
In the cupboard. Something's decaying
Under that glittering dress.

It was nearly ten years ago
We opened the gates. Since yesterday it seems
They have marched through our hearts like vandals
In a public park, swinging pick-axe handles
At the young saplings, dancing on the flower beds,
Pissing in the water gardens. Even our dreams
They have invaded, dragged the nightmares from our heads,
And put them on public show.

Ideas we thought were dead
They have exhumed, and like living corpses
With breath like cemeteries and faces decayed
They spread their diseases in our streets, parade
Lividly through our precincts, gatecrash our parties
And invite themselves to dinner, bore us with stories
Of their children's marvellous schools, how the house's
Trebled in value. We nod

With glazed eyes, saying nothing.
How can you speak to the morally dead
Who laugh at the very word community,
And damn the notion of equality
Between man and man, with a dismissive sneer?
Like people who live in graveyards, we tread
Carefully between oozing tombs, for fear
That we too are decaying.

Things we thought disgusting
They have made respectable. Words
We thought never to hear again, they shout
In our faces like abusive children. No doubt
Levers at the lid of that closed mind.
With no more intellectual substance than the birds'
Singing, and none of its beauty, who can find
Melody in such twittering?

Fellows who wear red braces
And striped shirts, perhaps; hard-faced girls
Who drive Ferrarris, and wear designer clothes;
People with sharp fingers, who have a nose
For money, and know the bread is buttered
On both sides if you catch it as it falls;
People who live in advertisements, within shuttered
Windows that shadow their faces

And shadow our consciences too.
We let it happen. What in us,
What darkness in our hearts, opened the gates
To these destroyers? What creates
The destroying instrument itself? Our dreams
Were cracked somewhere, there was pus
Gathering under the skin. What seems
Like lying, must have been true

In some sense at least. Shame
Squeezes our hearts: the knowledge that we
Were the generation of these living dead,
And worse, like a funeral bell in the head
Tolling us towards their graveyard, the thought
That we must destroy the brutal simplicity
Of their thinking, or admit defeat,
Acknowledging we are the same.

The uncivilised face in the mirror
Cannot be mine. That bloodshot eye,
That slobbering lip and acquisitive jaw,
That joyous boot that relishes nothing more
Than kicking, that's some other fellow
Not me, surely? I reject the lie
That this face is universal, as a shallow
And essentially vulgar error.

Learning to live in a city
Ruled by barbarians, knowing the conquest
Was wished, not suffered, corrodes
The heart like rust. The public roads
Gape with pot holes, the tarmac's cracking.
Municipal buildings are crumbling to dust.
Our floorboards shiver, the ceiling is falling.
We deserve someone's pity.

But there will be none. Our future
We shall create as we created the past.
This animal within, this destroyer,
This carnivore must be tamed, or we'll never
Live anything but merciless predators' lives.
Something more gentle, somewhere in the vast
Manslaying wilderness patiently survives:
A loving, human creature.

1989 -1992

Epistle to Louis Marks

I only have to lift the phone. Speaking
To you was never the Kafkaesque big deal
Some TV Producers delight in: meaningless eating
Of overpriced meals in jabbering restaurants, the whole
Phone performance - *he's in a meeting, busy,*
Out of the building, other line, at lunch
Give me your number we'll ring you back, sorry -.
They never do, of course, till the paranoid hunch
That you are being rubbished, becomes sober certainty
And you stop trying. That was never your game,
Or not with me. On the integrity
Scale, courtesy, like remembering the name
Of the person you're talking to, doesn't rate
With the principal virtues. It's not always the best
People who are the most considerate.
But as courtesy, so integrity: the rudest generally have least.

I still have the number, though it may have changed,
As almost everything else has, since the time
We were constantly talking, in that deranged
Semi-mania and semi-dream
Called television production. But I'd rather write
These Horatian quatrains, defend or attack
All the old bastions and targets, re-fight
Those last lost battles alone. You can't answer back
When I'm holding the pen. The time for dialogue
Has passed. Now we give evidence,
Enter our plea, write the epilogue,
Attempt to compel experience into sense.

We met by chance. Neither of us meant
To be television people, you an ex-scholar,
Ex-Marxist, Gramsci expert, and spent
Socialist like the rest of us: me a former
Enfant terrible knocking forty, marching
Staunchly in the opposite direction
From everybody else, determinedly making
Television dramas a dwindling population
Actually wanted to see, dreaming terse
Plays that were poems, poems that were dreams
Of plain speaking to an empty universe
Of what we might become. What seems
Like planning was probably chance, and policies
Consciously launched, manifestos stated,
Not worth the breath or paper. Our enemies
Held all the power cards. While we debated
Culture and mass society, the responsible stance
Of the National Theatre of the Air, the dramatic needs
Of all our people, they saw the chance
Of selling mediocrity to millions. Our culture bleeds
Now, its life seeps away into the earth.
They played their trumps and won. Politics,
Economic change, the zeitgeist, the birth,
Baptism and deification of greed as the public's
Official pantheon and philosophy
Did for our hopes. Technology too,
Dishes, tape machines, the ability
To choose, and choose badly. We both knew
We were likely to lose, but it didn't mean
The job wasn't worth doing, or better not done.
The statement must be made, the evidence seen
Before the frog march and the executioner's gun.

Now that it is over, what does it mean,
That experience we shared? How to avoid
Terminal conclusions, the feel of the clean
Blade at the throat, the abyss, the void
Opening beneath our feet: the fall
Further than Milton's angels into a vast
Uninhabited Universe, where all
That can be heard is silence, and the past
Present and future are all seen as one
Incomprehensible starstruck wilderness? That
Vision of judgement, or this: the fun
World, the brain-dead grin, the flat
Answer to the bland question, the Accountant's shirt,
Striped, like his judgement, the Banker's briefcase, the blunt
Hatchet man's reply: further into the dirt
For cash, cold violence, hot cunt?

It was another path we followed, Ariadne's thread
Into the cavern where the Minotaur
Lurked in his stink, and the dead
Remnants of a thousand virgins strewed the floor,
Fragmented Athenian hopes. In that chamber
Something like truth was demonstrated,
And we both sought to squeeze and clamber
Through to that cave to observe the sated
Blood-soaked beast in his lair. The image
Will stand for many horrors, personal, social,
Political. Predator and victim, sage
And acolyte, godhead and devotional
Worshippers: power in the state,
Rulers and ruled, the permanent tragedy
Of Government, the triumph of hate
Over love, gentleness, integrity.

What else were we trying to dramatise
While those ranks of advertisers and money men
Surrounded us like the glittering eyes
Of a savage and merciless barbarian
Army in the dark? They knew what to do
With the likes of us, what Goths and Vandals
Did to civilised villas and temples, screw
Plunder and burn, rip all the handles
From the ornamented doors, deface the walls,
Solve the cultural question with answering fire,
Leave roofless tenements, burned out halls,
A degraded city of sty and byre.
Tin gods now stand in place of stone,
Writing gives place to hieroglyph and scribble.
Nothing is left standing. The poets are gone.
Barbarian culture is scrawl and rubble.

Apocalyptic images, visions of doom
Too pretentious maybe for our ten years bled
Raw, trying to make plays for the common room
Of society, so what was thought and said
By the best of the dead and living should be seen
In our college's public living space
On the universal democratic screen,
That two way mirror where the multiform face
Of our society could view itself
And study its own blemishes: our people's voice
Speaking in its many tongues, the broad shelf
Where all our videos could stand together and choice
Would have some meaning, not a selection of the worst
But the incomprehensible variety of the best.
But the market researchers got there first
And all such hopes were soon laid waste.

We always enjoyed glooming, the bleak
Shake of the head, the dispirited sigh
As things slid further week by week
And decline sloped into years. We didn't lie
In those communal glooms. The Sybilline leaves,
The hoarse oracles, got it about right:
The cemetery is full of graves.
The Seventh Cavalry is not in sight.

These bleak Horatian elegiacs suit
My retrospective mood, as they do yours,
Perhaps: though the latter is a moot
Point, I know. Charlatans and whores
Surround you still, while I am in the clear.
Perhaps these verses should remain unread:
Tomorrow will come, next week, next year.
Some of our tapes may live when we are dead.

June-July 1992

15

On the morning after the 1992 Election

Old Wordsworth would be pleased, would have voted
Tory himself presumably. The young poet,
Before love and separation and a revolution carted
To the guillotine disjointed him, would have seen it
As a wasting of our powers more wholesale and complete
Than anything he could imagine, a crushing of nature
In the vice of commerce, an acceptance of defeat
The more fearful because welcomed as a hope for the future.
Milton, whom he invoked, would have understood.
A servile nation too corrupt for liberty
Would seem familiar to him. He would observe
That where there is no moral or spiritual food
People will starve, that the civil virtue is honesty,
And nations get the governments they deserve.

April 10th 1992

Lachrymae

It was a kind of religion.
It had its holy book, its sages,
Its punishments and rewards. To those
Who followed the determined road, and chose
To become part of the vision
It ordered and explained their lives, offered
Peace of a sort. Whatever outrages
Of spirit or flesh it committed, were suffered
With a martyr's conviction.

There were temples too, of a kind.
Only initiates could enter there,
And the rituals were secret, mysteries
Of power and confession, agonies
Of the body or within the mind
Too holy to be explained. There were hints of blood
Running under the door, a shiver of fear
Sensed, if not fully understood.
We weren't completely blind.

The collapse was sudden and dramatic.
No one had believed for years, the faith
That moves mountains and builds temples was dead.
Only the theology survived, structures in the head
Intricate and hieratic,
A language unbelievers could afford to speak
Without too much embarrassment. The truth
Was too violent to be acknowledged, it would break
Too much. Uncertain, agnostic,

We could only imagine the fall
Of such huge pediments and columns ages
Into the future. But the statues buckled
At the knees, the prisons gasped, and crumbled,
People danced on the wall
Of the temple precinct, hacking it with hammers
For souvenirs, shredding the sacred pages,
Jeering in the street at bureaucrats and dreamers,
Daubing the cathedral

Of the institutionalised truth
With obscenities and poems and tags.
The imagination rioted in the streets, the temples
Slid almost apologetically into dust, their lintels
Disintegrated, the rotten mouth
Of their foundations gaped for all to see.
What a facade it was! What rags
Those priests were wearing! How suddenly
The high flyers fell to earth!

In the beginning was the dream.
On cold uplands shivering ploughmen
Marvelled at the opening clouds, prisoners
Forgotten beneath the foundations, miners
In the darkest, narrowest seam
Imagined it as light. For slaves
And the persecuted, it meant hope, how men
Could imagine survival even at the grave's
Brink: somewhere, sometime.

By whatever particular name
That holy city was known, justice
Was its guiding principle, equality the rule.
For the temporary tenants of earth the school
Of wisdom taught the same
Simple curriculum, that brotherly sharing
Was better than greed, that enough could suffice
For all, that the Golden Age was sleeping,
Not dead, the millennium would come.

Reason, the brightest, cleverest,
Most glittering of the gods, would master
His shaggy brother, the shambling, instinctive
Tyrant of the dark heart, the destructive,
Loving, indispensable beast
Who shares power within. For sure,
Supremacy must pass to the higher creature,
The shaper, the maker, or what are visions for,
That sweating, creative unrest

That will not be content
With what is, but inhabits castles of what might be?
Love, like the fire at the heart of the universe,
Energises that vision, a practical, terse,
Unromanticised statement
Of the common dilemma, a holding hands
In time, an affirmation that our destiny
Is shared, something everyone understands
In the private continent

Of being, that secret country
Where we rule in solitude, king and subject.
That was Adam's second dream, after the fall,
Not the lost garden, but the living temple
Of New Jerusalem, the city
Of justice and love, where all exiles are at home.
Shall we wake and find it true? What object
Can the imagination create so morally supreme,
Or of such lasting beauty?

But then the fact, the wakening
To a cold morning, where nothing is given
And everything must be made, by hand
From the local stone. The unresponsive land
Must be planted, the building
Dug, from the foundations up. Hard sweat
On earth, no convenient heaven
To reach for. Dreams must be set
In concrete, visions become planning.

So now the drawing board,
Set square, straight edge and calculator,
So that the beautiful abstractions, equality,
Justice, the architecture of honesty
Drawn in the studio, make hard
Outlines of feasible buildings, policies
Of love in action, simulator
In the real world of the imagined societies
Of philosopher and bard.

And here the errors begin.
Belief to become living must give birth
To ideology, which will co-opt power
To enact its vision. The city requires a tower
To guard it, and somewhere within
That necessary building there is always a prison
For the enemies of the dream. Bitter earth
Stained with blood and tears, the risen
Spectre of original sin,

That theft in Paradise
Where everything was free, and only the realisation
Of ownership could liberate the snake
Of greed, the serpent of self, and break
The pattern of innocence. The vice
Tightens by generations, brother
Murders brother, the arts of desolation
Aspire to the sublime, and hell freezes over
With unforgiving ice.

Every liberator
Of the human spirit has a twin brother
With keys in his hand. As one swings back
The door to the house of freedom, his dark
Sibling, the incarcerator,
Double locks the cell, dreams of a time
Of universal perimeters, ever greater
Lubiankas of the spirit, every action a crime,
Every citizen a traitor.

The study of history,
That most liberating of disciplines,
Convinces no-one. Every vision,
Every disaster, is its own creation,
An unresolved mystery
As unique as a genetic fingerprint.
From experience we learn nothing. Sins
And saintliness, apparently, still point
The moral of the story.

A double-featured man
Haunts more than Europe. One face
Is radiant, seeing in the imagination
The beauty of the possible, the revolution
Of love, the street plan
Of Jerusalem. The other's narrow cheeks
And pursed lips image the disgrace
Of a species that must be disciplined, he speaks
The language of index and ban.

Yet the same narrow men
Who closed the theatres, opened minds
For ten generations, saw futures
Of visionary landscapes and loving creatures
To make the beast in his den,
The bloody patron of jailer and killer
Howl with rage. The same chain that binds
The seer to the slayer, handcuffs the slayer
To the visionary *when?* -

Compels the bloodcurtained eye
Of the Minotaur in his stinking cave
To recognise his destroyer, and the thread
That leads to the land of the living from the dead.
Hopes, like men, will die
More or less bloodily. The ogre will stand
Behind the dreamer's shoulder, ready to deprave
Every freedom into tyranny, and brand
On the forehead of truth its lie.

But behind each despair
As it bends to plunder the piled corpses
Of our murdered hopes, another hope
Rises from among the dead. We cope
With our three o' clock fear
As the Puritan soldiers coped with defeat:
This day was theirs, but the sun rises
Again tomorrow. We will not retreat.
Build Jerusalem here!

How should we try to live
When Utopia has been privatised
And re-opened as a Theme Park? Now
The tourists come to gawp at how
We held out our hands to give
And saw them chopped off at the wrists. School
Parties stroll past the exhibits unsurprised
By what they see. The images fall
Through their heads like earth from a sieve.

See these crucified slaves
Who rose against Roman rule, lining
The Appian Way like poplar trees.
We follow our written itineraries
To the next debacle. It saves
Time and too much thought. *Now see
The Roundheads who murdered their saintly King,
The tyrants who buried liberty
In one of its many graves.*

*This tableau, of course, is France,
Robespierre, the guillotine, the terror.
'Bliss was it in that dawn,' the poet said,
Before he had seen a single severed head.
After the briefest glance
In the basket, he ran home to nurse.
He preferred Old Corruption to such a horror.
Liberty always leads to something worse
Given half of half a chance.*

*And now our prize display !
Lenin the cynic, Trotsky the inept,
And the yellow-eyed climber with the cockroach moustache
Who built a prison so vast and so harsh
It blasted his people away
Like a maniac dynamiting a mountain. Ignore
That tearful young man who has just crept
Behind the scenery to weep. He's been before.
He comes here to cry every day.*

For the many dead he weeps,
For the murdered Communards and Old Bolsheviks,
For Sans Culottes, Levellers and Slaves
In their scattered, unmourned graves.
A kind of faith he keeps
With the visions they lived for, the power
Of the idea that can't be killed. It sticks
In the mind like a song sung in the darkest hour
While the world unquietly sleeps.

December 91 - August 92

Reunion in Sarajevo

They meet regularly, the dark-robed women.
The time and place
Of the next meeting is never known,
Only that there will be one.
The ancient disgrace
Will be re-enacted, the old moan
By the fresh earth, the white face
That says everything and nothing: and always a boy
Broken on the stones of Troy.

It was the Athenians who first troubled the graves
Of the dark-robed dead.
Triremes cut the unprotected waves
To Melos: the decree leaves
Nothing male living: the boys bleed
With the men, the women rostered as slaves.
And Hecuba stirs in her dark bed,
Andromache's ashes gather, Cassandra's lust
For prophecy is born again in the dust.

They have lost count now, the dark-robed mourners,
Of the many times they have met.
Fresh blood draws them, injustice gathers
These shadowy ladies, so that whatever suffers
Shares the remembrance of suffering, the wet
Cheeks, the torn hair, the terrors
Repeated again and again. They meet
Always in the hope that this will be the last
Reunion, that they may return in peace to the past:

Always disappointed. In the mortared market place
Andromache shovels her son
Into a bag. Raped Cassandra's crazed face
Stares from the TV screen. No trace
Of Polyxena's tomb. Dog-like, Hecuba digs alone
In the shelled graveyard. No peace
For the mutilated child-body, thrown
Into a cellar and burned. No identification:
An unknown daughter of a murdered nation.

They stand silently, the dark-robed women,
Heads leaning together in mourning.
No words can express their centuries of pain,
Only brushing of hands and cheeks, the fallen
Beauty of having seen too much, sensing
Too keenly that it will happen again.
They depart to their temporary graves, knowing
The next reunion is pencilled: only who will destroy
Is still uncertain, and what particular Troy.

June 1994

Don Taylor has worked as a playwright in all the media, theatre, television and radio, and has also directed nearly one hundred plays, working in all three forms.

His career began in 1960 as a drama director with BBC Television and during the sixties he did some of the most striking television productions of the age, directing the first six plays of David Mercer, with whom he had a close working relationship, described in his book, **Days of Vision**.

During the late seventies and most of the eighties he directed a series of large scale Theatre Classics on Television, ranging from Greek Tragedies to Edward Bond, and seven original television plays of his own, including **The Testament of John**, the only television drama to be written in verse.

He continued to write poetry during this period, as well as plays for the stage, which have been presented in London and in theatres all over the country. **When the Barbarians Came** is his fifteenth stage play to achieve production, and, including radio and television plays, his fiftieth overall.

Of his published plays, **The Roses of Eyam** and **The Exorcism** are very widely performed, and his Greek Tragedy translations, in verse, have become very popular and are staged all over the English speaking world.

He is married to playwright Ellen Dryden, and they have a daughter and a son.

ISBN 0 9524159 0 9